TIMELESS MELODIES

A NOSTALGIC COLLECTION OF CLASSIC SONG LYRICS

ROBERT DENNIS

978-1-965552-26-1 (Paperback)

Library of Congress Control Number: 2025906221

BOOKWRIGHTS
HOUSE

admin@bookwrightshouse.com
12211 W Washington Blvd.
Suite 110, Los Angeles CA 90066

I Love You Like An Addict

I love you like an addict
I can't get enough of you
I want you all the time
You are always on my mind

With both arms tight around me
It really completely makes my day
I think of you all the time
I can't think of anything else

You just control my mind
I am glad you are mine
I can't think of life without you
Cause I just live for you

You are the happiness that I have
There is nothing else for me
I love you like an addict
There is nothing else I want

I am glad when you are near me
When you are not I am lost
I don't know what to do

I Will Do Any Thing For You

I have loved you for a long time
I am so glad that you are mine
Let me tell you what I would do
I will do anything for you

I will wash the dirty dishes I will even sweep the floor
If that will not be enough
I will do even much more

I will do whatever you say
And I will do it your way
I will even wash your new car
And then tune up your guitar

Great you can fix the storm door
In time before the coming rain
That's on my list for tomorrow
You may have to tell me again

I will even take you shopping
And buy you a new set of clothes
I will take you some nice place to eat
I'd even buy you a parakeet

I will do whatever you say
And I will do it your way
I will even wash your new car
And then tune up your guitar

Robert Dennis

I Have Been A Fool For Ten Years

I have been a fool for ten years
I sat at home drowning in tears Met a girl that
changed my attitude
Now thank God I have be rescued

Just one night with Anna Lee Made me a
different me
Her voice whispering in my ear Realized I'd
been a fool ten years

I could have been out every night
Holding some body close and tight
I could have forgotten my tears
I have been a fool for ten years

We are living like we are cool Watching the
sunset by the pool Forgot the misery and tears
I was a fool for ten years

For ten years she left me all alone
I've been waiting, but she is still gone

I could have been out every night
Holding some body close and tight
I could have forgotten my tears
I have been a fool for ten years

I Couldn't Love You More If I Tried

I recall when you were the blushing bride No one in the
crowd eyes were dry I couldn't love you more if I tried
Then when we held each other-and cried

When I carried you into our first home
I knew nothing would ever be the norm
I couldn't love you more if I tried
Then when we held each other-and cried

Everything was just okay
For our little girl first birthday
I couldn't love you more if I tried
Then when we held each other-and cried

You know I have loved you all my life
And you have been a wonderful wife
I couldn't love you more if I tried
Then when we held each other-and cried

They Call Me Temptation

I had been working over time
I stopped for a glass of wine
Only one other person was there
The most beautiful girl I'd seen

I went over and ask her name
She said my real name is Elain
But my friends call me Temptation
It was natural that I ask why

She said ever thing that I do
They will try to do it too
If I want to dance all night
Or if I bungee jump off the bridge

Or if I speed down the highway
They try to pass say, it makes their day
If I skinny dip in the moon lite
That's is just their biggest delight

Looking into her pretty eyes
I knew she could cast a spell
So I just wished her well
And then I said my goodbye

Everyone Knows I Love You

It is very plain to see No one knows who I am
No one knows what I do
Everyone knows I love you
And that you love me too

They know by the smile on my face
Seeing my arms around you
And me kissing your sweet lips
And the sparkle in your eyes
And that you love me too

They know how I make you laugh
The way we are holding hands
While walking side by side
With the pep in my step
And that you love me too

It is very plain to see
No one knows who I am
No one knows what I do
Everyone knows I love you
And that you love me too

If I Never Had Known You

My life would not have been complete
If we had not the chance to meet
I would regret it all my whole life thru
If I never had known you

I would have missed this happiness
And the loving touch of your caress
And the loving things that we can do
If I never had known you

If I never had known you
There's no telling where I'd be
I'd be like the driftwood on the sea
If I never had known you
You are the strength I lean upon
You're the sweetest love I've ever known
And my happy days would have been too few
If I never had known you

If I never had known you
My life would be only emptiness
In place of all this happiness
If I never had known you

If I never had known you
I would be in this world alone
I would never had made a home
If I never had known you

There Is Nothing You Can Do That Will Stop Me From Loving You

Our love is a wonderful thing
I never want it to change
There is nothing you can do
That will stop me from loving you

I know that you could cheat and lie
And you could try to make me cry
There is nothing you can do
That will stop me from loving you

You could run around all over town
And you could try to tear me down
There is nothing you can do
That will stop me from loving you

You can go ahead and try to hide
Do what you want, go ahead and try
But there is nothing you can do
That will stop me from loving you

If you wanted to be free
Then you would have to leave
And if ever you do
I'll keep on living you

You could run around all over town
And you could try to tear me down
There is nothing you can do
That will stop me from loving you

You can go ahead and try to hide
Do what you want, go ahead and try
But there is nothing you can do
That will stop me from loving you

Oh there is nothing you can do
That will stop me from loving you

That Vase

I saw her and admired God's creation
I loved her thru her cremation
In my heart she will always have a place
But all that's left of her is in that vase

I see her eyes as blue as the sky
Eyes that were never meant to cry
And her soft blonde hair that frames her face
But all that's left of her is in that vase

I wonder will we ever meet again
So we can walk again hand in hand
Somewhere in that heavenly space
Now all that's left of her is in that vase

I set and stare at what used to be
But there is nothing left here but me
And I wonder what could have been
If things were different back then

I wonder will we ever meet again
So we can walk again hand in hand
Somewhere in that heavenly space
Now all that's left of her is in that vase

I look forward to that heavenly place
Where I expect to find an empty vase

ROBERT DENNIS

Let Me Tell You

By Bobby Dennis

Let me tell you where I have been
I have been to the palace of Queens
It is the best place to be seen
Met the pretties girl you've ever seen

Blonde hair the color of the Sun
And she say's blondes do have more fun
She has eyes as blue as the sky
Lips as red and sweet as cherry pie

I told you about Sherry
Let me tell you about me
I am in love so much
I can't tell which way is up

She says that she really loves me
Wants a family of two or three
We are going to settle down
In a big house outside of town

Let me tell you about last night
No I think that will be our secret

I Have A Real Good Heart

I have a real good heart
That's a good place to start
You can live like a queen
And have all the good things

All you just have to do is love me like I love you
And give me your heart
And we will never be apart
When nights are long and cold

And you need someone to hold I'll be there with open
        arms
You will never come to any harm
I have a real good heart
It has never been broken apart

It was made for loving you
And it is as good as new
All you just have to do is love me like I love you
And give me your heart
And we will never be apart

I Have Had A Good Life

It is good to see you today
And you are back in town to stay
Oh, yes I have had a good life
Been better with you as my wife

I have had a good life
With no trouble or strife
Time has been good to you
So now what do we do

Your husband died of a heart attack
You know my wife died in a car wreck
And now you are back on your own I am the only one at home
You chose the finer things in life

Although I wanted you for my wife
Some things are meant to, or not to be
I wonder about you and me
I have had a good life

With no trouble or strife
Time has been good to you
So now what do we do
There is no need to complain

Because it wouldn't change a thing
I have had a good life
With no trouble or strife
Time has been good to you
So now what do we do

Did You Hear What I Hear

I hear you really like me
And that's a joy to my car
And you really like it here
And did you hear what I hear

I am talking to my self
Wishing what I hear is true
About what I hear about you
And my search for love is thru

Here is what I hope that your hear That is, I really
     love you
And I am ready to say I do
I am wishing that you are too
I am talking to my self

Wishing what I hear is true
About, what I hear about you
And my search for love is thru
Did you hear what I hear?

And what I would like to do
I am talking to my self
Wishing what I hear is true
About what I hear about you
And my search for love is thru

All American Girl

She has, flowing flaming red hair
And her teeth are white as pearl
Her beautiful sparkling blue eyes
Will set your heart in a whirl
She's an all American girl

She has a mind of her own
She knows what she wants to do
She knows where she is going
She will make it in a man's world
She's an all American girl

She has her eyes on her goal
And has her plans well made
She is looking for the day
When she makes it in a man's world
She's an all American girl

She has flowing flaming red hair
And her teeth are white as pearl
Her beautiful sparkling blue eyes
Will set your heart in a whirl
She's an all American girl

She wants a career of her own
And a place she can call home

She has flowing flaming red hair
And her teeth are white as pearl
Her beautiful sparkling blue eyes
Will set your heart in a whirl
She's an all American girl

Just A Little Time

I've known you for just a little time
I know I want to make you mine
I know that I can win your love
Just as sure as there's stars above

Just spend a little time with me
Just a little time is all that I need
Just a little time to make up your mind
You will love me in just a little time

I know that we can work out a plan
So that I can be more than just a friend
So that I can love you until time shall end
I can prove it in just a little time

Just spend a little time with me
Just a little time is all I need
Just a little time, wait and see
Then I know that you'll love me

I'm A Thinker, Dreamer, And A Schemer

I'm a thinker, dreamer, and a schemer
I'm thinking I like all that I see
I think you would make a good lover
I'm thinking you are all that I need

I am dreaming about you right now
I'm dreaming about the future you and me
And about running my fingers thru your hair
I'm dreaming of you spending time with me

I'm scheming to get you into my arms
I'm scheming to kiss your lips and steal your charms
I'm scheming to steal your heart away
I'm scheming to make you mine forever and a day

I Crossed That River

I crossed that river deep and wide
My darling was on the other side
I could be holding her at this time
Here I sit in this slow moving line

This ferry boat moves so slow
Sometime we go with the flow
Sometime we get stuck in the sand
I on keep wishing we were on dry land

But I'll see my darling to night
I will kiss and hold her real tight
All of this is worth the pain
I've got to cross that river again

I Can't Wait Until Tomorrow

I've been gone for so long
Now I just want to take you home
I can't wait until tomorrow
I want to love you today

Now that I'm back home to stay
I'll wipe away all of your sorrow
I can't wait until tomorrow
I want to love you today

I want to hold you one more time
I want to feel your heart beat like mine
I can't wait until tomorrow
I want to love you to day

I want to taste the sweetness of your kiss
Make me know what I have missed
I can't wait until tomorrow
I want to love you today

Now that I'm back home to stay
I'll wipe away all of your sorrow
I can't wait until tomorrow
I want to love you today

You're Too Good To Be Bad

Can't believe the things that are said
The talk about you is not good
They say you would hurt me if you could
But you are too good to be bad

If I should loose you I'd be so sad
I love you for all the world to see
You are all the love I'll ever need
And you are too good to be bad

I trust you to do things that make me glad
The rumors I hear I don't believe
You have always been true to me
And you are too good to be bad

I'll never leave you or wish I had
With you is where I want to be
Your eyes and your kiss tell me
And you are too good to be bad

I trust you to do things that make me glad
The rumors I hear I don't believe
You have always been true to me
And you are too good to be bad

ROBERT DENNIS

Let's Fall In Love Again

The sky was a little more blue
Back when our love was new
Let's go back where we began
And let's fall in love again

I recall when we were together
How we would hold each other
And pray the night would never end
So let's fall in love again

I use to see the fire in your eyes
And we sure did make the sparks fly
It was a thrill to hold your hand
So let's fall in love again

We've been together for so long
Now all the sizzle is gone
Let's make us some more new plans
And let's fall in love again

We can have lots of fun
Cause we know how it's done
We just have to say when
So let's fall in love again

I Could Have Loved You

By Bobby Dennis

I see you on the street
It's too late for us to meet
If I had only know you
Then I could have loved you

I see you sitting over there
With a face so sweet and dear
If I had known you at 22
Then I could have loved you

I see you in the next lane
And I don't even know your name
I have seen many like you
I could have loved them too

Ever how many comes my way
I will just have to say
That the best I have ever known
Is the one I have at home

I Like Every Thing About You

By Bobby Dennis

I like the way you walk
I like the way you talk
I like your attitude
I like everything about you

I like the way you wiggle
I like the way you giggle
I like the way you wave your hand
I would like to be your man

I like the way you roll your hips
I like the way you puff your lips
I like your eyes of blue
I like everything about you

I like your dancing feet
I like your pearly white teeth
I like your red hair too
I like everything about you

I like the way you wiggle
I like the way you giggle
I like the way you wave your hand
I would like to be your man

There Is No Ring On Your Hand

By Bobby Dennis

There is no ring on your hand
Does that mean you have no man?
I've been looking for someone like you
I'll make you an offer you can't refuse

If you let me, I know I can
Put a gold ring on your left hand
Give you a car and money to spend
And a love that will never end

Since there is no ring on your hand
Let me tell you about my plan
We can have a house on the edge of town
We can live in a world of our own

If you let me I know I can
Put a gold ring on your left hand
Give you a car and money to spend
And a love that will never end

On Cloud Nine

I was on cloud nine
When I thought you were mine
I was walking on air
When I thought you cared

My feet didn't touch the ground
Whenever you were around
You had me flying so high
I should have known I couldn't survive

I was up among the stars
Now I'm down where you are
But how was I to know
You'd bring me down so low

It's just a game of love and leaving
You left me hurting and grieving
When you left me behind
And went away with a friend of mine

I was on cloud nine
When I thought you were mine
He will be sorry some day
Just like me he'll have to pay

You've Never Grown Old

I thought about you today
It's been so long since you went away
Time has always put your face on hold
In my mind you've never grown old

Life sure has changed since you went away
I remember just like yesterday
But you haven't changed with the times
You've never grown old, in my mind

I still picture your pretty face
No one has ever taken your place
I wished I could have seen you many times
You've never grown old, in my mind

I have missed you all these years
Sometime I have to wipe away a tear
Today I'm old and fading with the times
But you've never grown old, in my mind

Reasons To Live

By Bobby Dennis

I had nothing to live for
But fate has opened a door
I had lost all I ever had
Everything looked so bad

I had nothing left to give
You gave me reasons to live
But when you held me so tight
I knew everything was right

I had never had such a thrill
You gave me reasons to live
It's like heaven when we meet
You're like an angel at my feet

As I gaze into your blue eyes
Its then I come to realize
I had never know love so real
You have given me reasons to live

But when you held me so tight
I knew everything was right
I had never had such a thrill
You gave me reasons to live

I've Lived To Love Another Day

By Bobby Dennis

I thought that I would surely die
The day that you told me good bye
But now I am happy to say
I've lived to love another day

It seemed like such a crazy world
Til I met this wonderful girl
She gave me all you took away
And I've lived to love another day

I look forward to each new dawn
So I can spend more time in her arms
She has changed my life so many ways
And I've loved to love another day

I thought I was through with love
But now I can't get enough
She is in my life to stay
And I've lived to love another day

The Second Time Around

By Bobby Dennis

I was sad when you went away
I am glad you are back to stay
I'll use all that I have learned
To welcome your return

I loved you very much before
Now I love you even more
Nothing better have I found
Then loving you the second time around

Gone is all that bitterness
The second time is the sweetest
And I won't let you down
Loving you the second time around

I know this time will last
My heart is beating fast
Just listen to that sound
Of loving you the second time around

I loved you very much before
Now I love you even more
Nothing better have I found
Then loving you the second time around

Heart Don't Listen

By Bobby Dennis

Heart don't you listen to him
He is only passing thru
And he is only using you
Til he finds another to fool

He will only do you wrong
And then he will be gone
You will be left all alone
With no shoulder to cry on

Heart don't listen to his line
If his lips are moving he's lying
And he will just leave you crying
So tell him you are not buying

Heart don't listen to his sweet words
Or anything he has to say
You will live to see better days
So just turn and walk away

He will only do you wrong
And then he will be gone
You will be left all alone
With no shoulder to cry on

I Thought I Had Seen It All

I have seen everything in the East
And I have been all over the West
I just thought I had seen it all
That was until the day I saw you

I saw it all and was ready to quit
There was something I hadn't seen yet
The most beautiful thing in my life
The beautiful girl who became my wife

I have been there, seen China's great wall
And I thought I had seen it all
At least all the worlds very best
Until I saw you in your wedding dress

I just knew I had seen it all
But then I just stood still in awe
I had seen nothing in the world
Compared to you and our baby girl

There is no telling what the future holds
So maybe I haven't seen it all

I saw it all and was ready to quit
There was something I hadn't seen yet
The most beautiful thing in my life
The beautiful girl who became my wife

I Am A Survivor

I am a survivor of a million heart aches
All because of my and some ones mistakes
I have survived a lot of lonely years
And with no one there to care

I am a survivor
But what am I surviving for
I am still alive and free
Maybe there is still hope for me

I am a survivor of an ocean of tears
That I have shed thru the years
Sometimes I just wanted to die
But all I did was hurt and cry

I am a survivor of broken dreams
And a hundred other schemes
I just can't understand
Why I didn't fit in a good plan

I am a survivor
But what am I surviving for
I am still alive and free
Maybe there is still hope for me

I Haven't Forgotten You

Nice that you remember me
This is the day you set me free
When I didn't want you to
No I haven't forgotten you

Or the worst day of my life
And all the pain you caused me
And all the hell you put me thru
No I haven" for gotten you

We had a beautiful life
But you threw that all away
The day you found someone new
No I haven't forgotten you

I remember, the good times
But you tore my world apart
Guess I was too easy to fool
And I haven't forgotten you

No I haven't found someone new
And I haven't gotten over you

We had a beautiful life
But you threw that all away
The day you found someone new
No I haven't forgotten you;

You Are The Other Woman

I can't see you like I want to
You live on the other side of town
We would be seen hanging around
And you would be the other woman

I don't hold you like I would
It might not be understood
Folks would say I am your man
And you would be the other woman

Gossip is like news, it is spread around
You know how they talk in this town
And it doesn't matter if it is truth
And no one will check it out

I can't kiss you like I used to
There is too much gossip around
You know how it is in this town
And you would be the other woman

We can't dance together again
I can only do that in my mind
I wish I could do that again
But you would be the other woman

Gossip is like news, it is spread around
You know this is a nosey town
And it doesn't matter if it is truth
And no one will check it out

I Loved You More Than He Did

When you left and went away
You knew I loved you every day
You chose him over me instead
But I loved you more than he did

You said for me to go away I told you
I loved you every day
You said you wanted him instead
But I loved you more than he did

I'm always happy to see you
But there is nothing I can do
I have someone to whom I belong
Waiting for me back at home

It was such a terrible day
You wouldn't listen to what I say
You turned me away and I cried
And it was our last goodbye

Now that you are on your own
I'll lend you a shoulder to cry on
I have loved you since I was a kid
I always loved you more than he did

I'm always happy to see you
Bur there is nothing I can do
I have someone to whom I belong
Waiting for me back at home

Hard Headed Woman

Back when I met this young woman
I thought would be the love of my life
For a while everything was alright
So she agreed to be my wife

For a while everything was just fine
Then I think she changed her mind
Now everything is going wrong
If it is not going her way

Her way is always the right way
It is her way or no way
Won't agree with anything I say
Or anything I plan to do
She would run the world if she could

But it would have to be her way
All would have to agree .but they wouldn't
They would all want to have their say
She is just a hard headed woman

It may not be any better
But it surely would be different
She is a hard headed woman
You cannot tell her anything

She Is The Only One That Wanted Me

Number one said I was too poor
That she couldn't live the way I do
She wanted to party and to have fun
She said I worked too much and had none

Number two said I was too unknown
That it would bring her status down
Time and chance has change both around
It's like a new way of life was found

We have lived a life of love
By the help of our God above
And have for a very long time
Because I am hers and she is mind

We are not poor and are well known
And we have made it here on our own
Here we are for the whole world to see
Our lives together are now history

We have lived a life of love
By the help of our God above
And have for a very long time
Because I am hers and she is mind

The Love Of Our Lives

I saw this lovely woman setting along
So I walked over and sat beside her
I told her my name and ask for hers
I said you looked so alone I came to help

I asked what is your dream and plans
She said I always wanted to be some ones wife
And to have a family of our own
You won't believe it that is also mine

We ought to get to gather and talk
We may be able to solve both problems
We began to see each other often
We discussed all our hopes and plans

To see how we could make them happen
We both already had working jobs
We gest how much a house would cost
And what would be the monthly expenses

And what to do about transportation
And what our family would think
We decided that it would not matter
So we decide to get married now

That was the best decision of our lives
We have been the love of our life
And plan it to be the rest of our life

That Is Where I Will Be

I have traveled around this world
All my life I have just roamed
For a long time away from home
I've seen places I would like to own

I've seen the world at its best
I've seen the world at its worst
I have seen most of the rest
And some I never want to see again

I don't recall every place I've been
But where the people are good
And the weather is better
That is where I want to be

I have missed a lot at home
And lots of times I've been alone
And if I can travel all night
I will be home by morning light

There is nothing better than being free
Than to be with the folks that love me
So by the time of morning light
That is just where I will be

I don't recall every place I've been
But where the people are good
And the weather is better
That is where I want to be

The One At Home

I set here in this lobby
And watch pretty girls go by
Thinking I could have loved them
But I didn't know them back then

They come from many places
And come from different races
And all are easy on the eyes
And they come in different sizes

Some act if they are looking
Some as this is where they're from
I'm not looking, just watching
I have a good one at home

Some come in large or small groups
And some will come all alone
But the one who loves me
Is the one I have at home

Some could be a star of a show
Some could be a CEO
But the one that I love
Is the one I have at home

I Have To Face Reality

I thought she would be back by now
I guess she will get by some how
But I am not so sure about me
Guess I have to face reality

She doesn't even answer her phone
Looks like I'm going to be alone
She doesn't want to talk to me
Guess I have to face reality

Crying won't bring her back again
This is not a game I can win
She doesn't want me it's plain to see
Guess I have to face reality

Looks like I am wasting these tears
And she doesn't see and doesn't care
It's time to get up off my knees
Guess I have to face reality

I Never Want To Hear That Name

I never want to hear that name
Because it brings me so much shame
She was the only thing on my mind
That is what makes love so blind

She threw me down for some other fool
She treated me so very cruel
I want to make it very plain
I never want to hear that name

I was working day and night
And she wasn't treating me right
She was out partying all the time
I never want to hear that name

I never want to hear that name
It brings memories that cause me pain
I was such a fool to believe
That she ever really loved me

She threw me down for some other fool
She treated me so very cruel
I want to make it very plain
I never want to hear that name

I Think I'm In Love With A Memory

It's been so long since we were together
She said she would be gone forever
I remember when she was here with me
I think I'm in love with a memory

I know now that she is really gone
And I am here all alone
And I should be happy and free
I think I'm in love with a memory

I don't know how she looks today
I remember when she went away
Why does her memory still haunt me
I think I'm in love with a memory

I still remember her beautiful face
No one has been able to take her place
Her leaving brought me such agony
I think I'm in love with a memory

I know now that she is really gone
And I am setting here all alone
And I should be happy and free
But I think I'm in love with a memory

Love The Hurt Away

By Bobby Dennis

There was someone before you
And she broke my heart into;
It still hurts, what else can I say
Please say you'll love the hurt away

I've been looking, hoping to find
Someone who's better this time
You will make this a better day
If you will love the hurt away

My life has been so full of pain
I thought I'd never smile again
Let me hold you and hear you say
That you will love the hurt away

I could have used you long ago
Before the tears began to flow
But now it is not too late
If you can love the hurt away

I've been looking, hoping to find
Someone who's better this time
You will make this a better day
If you will love the hurt a way

No Pain Like A Broken Heart

My woman left, I thought I could stand the pain
But it hurts over and over again
For relief I don't know where to start
I found there is no pain like a broken heart

I've been hurt over and over again
But this time I cannot explain
Stones and broken bones, had more than my part
But there is no pain like a broken heart

Back when I was in a car wreck
I wound up with a broken neck
Just had to take a lot of time
But everything turned out fine

The time when I had those kidney stones
I thought this time I am really gone
The pain brought me down to my knees
I just had to beg for relief

When that tooth made me walk the floor
I thought I just can't stand any more
No other pain can be this sharp
But I found no pain like a broken heart

I've been hurt over and over again
But this time I cannot explain
Stones and broken bones, had more than my part
But there is no pain like a broken heart

What Could Have Been

A drunk ran a traffic light
And it took her young life
She was just seventeen
With a head full of dreams

We will never know what could have been
He wanted to start a new life just right
Too much party late at night
He finished school with a four point O

What could have been we'll never know
We'll never know what could have been
We'll never know what could have been
But we'll always know just what should have been

What about a child that was never born
Never saw the light of its first morning
And that was no accident
We will never know what could have been

Who knows what life would hold
If they had lived to be old old old
Doctor lawyer or maybe president
We will never know what could have been

I Can't Erase Your Memory From My Mind

Today everything is done by machine
With one touch I can erase most any thing
I keep searching, hoping to find
One to erase your memory from my mind

So many places remind me of you
And the things we used to do
Like the places we used to dine
I can't erase your memory from my mind

I see someone with your hair style
Then I see another with your smile
I think it's just a waste of time
To try to erase your memory from my mind

So many things remind me of you
And of all the hurt I've been thru
I loved you for such a long time
Now I can't erase your memory from my mind

I Can't Help It If I Cry

The one I love has proved untrue
She left and never said why
My heart is breaking into
I can't help it if I cry

As I look at her paper face
And see her big blue eyes
I know another takes my place
I can't help it if I cry

Thro we'll always be a part
I can't forget her thro I try
Her memory makes the tear drops start
I can't help it if I cry

This loneliness I can't stand
I don't care if I live or die
This loneliness has no end
I can't help it if I cry

One More Step Before I Cry

I slowly walked away from the door
I know I'll never be here anymore
She just said this is our last good bye
I'll take one more step before cry

She hurt me more than she will ever know
But I won't ever let her see it show
She can't see how I'm hurting deep inside
I'll take one more step before I cry

One more step is all I'll take
What I need before I break
And it doesn't really matter if I try
My life is changing today

By the words she had to say
So I'll take one more step before I cry
I know that she's standing at the door
I know I'll never see her any more

She wanted to tears in my eyes
I'll take one more step before I cry
My whole world ended today
I never thought it would end this way

I will love her till the day I die
I'll take one more step before I cry
One more step is all I'll take
What I need before I break

And it doesn't really matter if I try
My life is changing today
By the words she had to say
So I'll take one more step before I cry

Yes I'll take one more step before I cry
Oh I'll take one more step then I'll cry

ROBERT DENNIS

Here Comes Grumpy

By Bobby Dennis

Here comes grumpy
Don't ask how he feels
He'll list every problem, from his head to his heels
They call him grumpy, it fits like a glove

He wouldn't be happy in heaven above
It doesn't matter if it's rain or shine
Whatever the weather you'll hear him whine
It doesn't matter if it is cold or hot

Because it won't suit him likely as not
He is bored in the day time and hates all his nights
You will never find one thing he likes
Here comes grumpy

Don't ask how he feels
He'll list every problem from his head to his heels
They call him grumpy it fits like a glove
He wouldn't be happy in heaven above

He leaves his home early to start out his day
But all the traffic gets in his way
The light may turn green but he won't go on
He usually sets there just bitch and moan
Not even once has he had a nice day

It best to stay out of his way
Here comes grumpy
Don't ask how he feels
He'll list every problem from his head to his heels

They call him grumpy it fits like a glove
He wouldn't be happy in heaven above
Wouldn't be happy in heaven above
Wouldn't be happy in heaven above

Cause he's grumpy

Some Times You Cross My Mind

I recall our graduation day
Every all went our separate way
I remember the class reunion in 89
Sometimes you cross my mind

I remember when the war came to an end
And the return of our best friend
That was the year I loved Caroline
Sometimes you cross my mind.

I remember your wedding day
And I watched as you rode away
I remember the stock market decline
And sometimes you cross my mind

The town got a new shopping mall
And we got a new park with a pool
We were sad when they closed the five and dime
Sometimes you cross my mind

I remember the championship game
And someone mentioned your name
True love has been so hard to find
Sometimes you cross my mind

Heartaches Tears And Ice Cold Beer

By Bobby Dennis

I stopped at the bar and grill
I asked is this for real?
I couldn't believe my eyes
They sat around and cried

I asked the waitress
What's the meaning of this?
They all come in here
To share Heartaches tears and ice cold beer

As I headed for the door
She said don't leave there'll be more
I said I don't believe I fit here
With Heartaches tears and ice cold beer

She said it's just not your turn
So I will save you this chair
And someday you will return
And share heartaches tears and ice cold beer

I Love Her She Loves Him

I can't change her mind
I've tried a hundred times
Why can't she just see?
She'd be better off with me

In this love affair
Is me verses them
Because I love her
She's in love with him

He doesn't intend to stay
Why can't he just go away?
He just a short time friend
He'll break her heart again

In this love affair
Is me verses them
Because I love her
She's in love with him

It's not the way it should be
I want her for only me
She should know he's no good
I love her more than he ever could

In this love affair
Is me verses them
Because I love her
She's in love with him

She's An Old Flame That Keeps Burning

My heart skips when I hear her name
I wonder if I can ever change
Her memory keeps returning
She's an old flame that keeps burning

I've tried to remove her from my mind
It doesn't work most of the time
Her memory keeps my mind churning
She's an old flame that keeps on burning

I close my eyes I see her in my sleep
I wonder what would happen should we meet
Would I just pass her by?
Or would I turn away and cry

Now that I'm living a new life
What would I tell my wife?
That her memory just keeps returning
And that she's an old flame that keeps burning

Fast Lane

It's Monday morning I'm late again
It's been another lost week end
I don't remember all that I did
All I have to show is a head ache

Here I sit in the fast lane
Nothing to show in my name
Traffic and my life are the same
Going nowhere in the fast lane

Once I had a wife and a girl friend
And I had money to spend
Now All I have is an apartment and bills
I'm sitting still in a leased automobile

And just a few good time friends
All the fun we have is just pretend
A nowhere job that I can't change
I'm stuck sitting still in the fast lane

My credit card is maxed out
My last check was an over draft
And it's driving me insane
That's life in the fast lane

Every Day Is A New Day

Every day is a new day
Meant to be better from what we've learned
So that we will know which way to turn
I can move on or I can stay

See that sun rise in the east
It's the beginning of a new day
So whatever comes your way
You need to give it your very best

Every day is a new day
Yesterday is already gone
So are some of its wrongs
A day to help someone on their way

Every day is a new day
Meant to be better than the one before
And so we can enjoy life more and more
And I like it this way

My Best Choice

My first choice was not you
There were others before you
I was hurt and didn't know what to do
My best choice was choosing you

There were others I had in mine
But they were wrong time after time
Life is not very much fun
When you have chosen the wrong one

You are not the one I wanted you to be
But you are the one that's good for me
Together we can make this life thru
My best choice was choosing you

When I think of the other ones
And the things we could have done
But you fit the things I plan to do
My best choice was choosing you

www.ingramcontent.com/pod-product-compliance
Lightning Source LLC
Chambersburg PA
CBHW061718120626
46550CB00003B/1274